T0354415

Discover what made St. Nicholas successful and have that Christmas feeling all the time!

***The Gifts of Nicholas* is a pretty and exceedingly positive book that will appeal to both believers and nonbelievers.**

The book is equal parts a celebration and a work with a mission. King writes for those who await the Christmas season with childlike enthusiasm; he also sets out to influence and encourage his audience to open their hearts and minds, to learn to give to others, and to exemplify the true spirit of the season.

The book compiles poetry and essays. The origin of St. Nicholas is addressed in the poems. Many well-known

Christmas song lyrics are incorporated, as with "on every street corner you can meet smile after smile, laughing all the way, bringing peace on earth."

Though it may seem perfect to read aloud to kids at Christmastime, the book definitely has a message for adults as well. Amid the interwoven poems and essays, a common theme and continuing story emerge. From the first-person perspective of a man living alone, interspersed essays tell a tale of unexpected contact.

A mystery begins to build when a mysterious wrapped gift is found, and it could only have been left by Santa. The narrator's parents and siblings are involved, as is a whole lot of wonder. From one Christmas to the next, the story grows, becoming even more amusing and life-changing. Disbelief turns into something else entirely. These believable essays are the meat of the book, and the poetry functions more as dressing around them.

The tone is pointed, calm, and alive with possibilities along this holiday journey. King's writing is clear and easy to understand. His message is about giving to others, feeling good, achieving your dreams, and enjoying a special time of year. "Christmas is that time of year when we celebrate our humanity and build it, contagiously," King writes. "I believe that Santa Claus is the physical manifestation of the spirit of Christmas … All those people who have written, sang, danced, or even dreamt about Christmas have … because that spirit has touched them inside."

The Gifts of Nicholas is a pretty and exceedingly positive book, holding appeal for children and adults, both those who believe and those who don't.

Reviewed by Billie Rae Bates (Clarion Review)

Goodreads Reviews:

Something total new! The combination of story telling and poetry is something extremely unique. The book is full of good messages, great for all ages. This is more than just a Christmas book it can be read anytime of year, and definitely should be read more than once! I highly recommend it to everyone.
-Anonymous

Recommends it for: young adults to adults inclusive.

A thought provoking book with beautiful poetry and essay form, bringing alive the spirit of giving. Our world needs to believe in Santa Claus to bring the goodness of love and joy where there is so much fear and hatred. The book made me realize that I am successful in so many ways in my daily life. A very good feel read.
-Anonymous

I was the lucky winner of a copy of this book through a Goodreads win. It is a very nice book about the feeling of Christmas. It contains 25 selections, some are in the form

of poems, others essays or letters and each one is thought provoking.
-Anonymous

This book really made me sit back and reflect. There is a variety of writing styles. I never thought I would enjoy reading poetry but this book has changes that.
-Anonymous

The Gifts of Nicholas

JAMES MARION KING

BALBOA.
PRESS
A DIVISION OF HAY HOUSE

Balboa Press books may be ordered through booksellers or by contacting:

Balboa Press
A Division of Hay House
1663 Liberty Drive
Bloomington, IN 47403
www.balboapress.com
1 (877) 407-4847

Print information available on the last page.

ISBN: 978-1-5043-9871-8 (sc)
ISBN: 978-1-5043-9873-2 (hc)
ISBN: 978-1-5043-9872-5 (e)

Library of Congress Control Number: 2018902297

Balboa Press rev. date: 03/22/2018

DEDICATION

To my daughter
Who makes her parents proud
Her courage contagious

To my son
Whom I have inspired
Who in turn inspires me

To the love of my life
Who opened my heart
And sings my song

To my parents
My sisters and brothers
They journey with me

To those who have taught
That I should learn

To all those who thought me watching
To all those who thought me listening
I definitely was

So many people have touched my life
And planted seeds
One such seed:

There are no such things as problems
There are only opportunities

This book is for all of you as you have shaped my way

Table of Contents

Success
His
Legacy

Christmas Can't Be Far Away

Once a year, every year, we decorate our lives with the spirit of Christmas. It is that special time of year when we open our hearts and rinse our minds. In this festive season, we treat all of our senses and delight as others do the same. Within these pages, you are invited to recall the joy and that special something Christmas has given to you.

Read each passage, enjoy each image, and create new and lasting memories. Learn more of Nicholas, the bishop of Myra, how he became such a boundless success. He can reach inside you, caress your heart, and share his magic, the magic that has now made one day each year very special. That one day has evolved into the Christmas season and more.

Saint Nicholas and Christmas touch us all. Even those who don't celebrate are affected by them. Some of their universal methods and tools of success and happiness are here for the learning, so that you might take them into your life. Use them to change or enhance your journey through life. Then you will know that Christmas can't be far away.

The Song of This Night

On this eve of joyous Noel,
Silhouettes flashed against the moon—
Reindeer, a sleigh, and the jolliest of elves.

In fine speed they swiftly passed,
Then faded softly into the night.
The jingling of bells I barely heard.

In my eyes the image abides.
Dare I admit this enchanting play?
I say aloud this is Santa's big scene.

On this eve of joyous Noel,
The story unfolds against the moon
Of reindeer, a sleigh, and the jolliest of elves.

Jolly old St. Nicholas.
The song of this night!

Christmas the Season

Kris Kringle, Kris Kringle, where are you tonight?
I've hung up my stocking for you in plain sight.
Please read my small letter I have sent you on white.
It has all my wishes to make my day bright.

Bring Rudolph, bring Rudolph, his nose glowing red.
He will fly through the night; his feet are not lead.
Please wake all your reindeer and take them from bed.
Put a team to your sleigh just like it is said.

Christmas tree, Christmas tree, your coat of dark green
All covered in tinsel and lit to be seen.
Now waiting for the gifts to finish your sheen.
In all of your splendor I am really quite keen.

The music, the music we sing from our hearts
That brings in the season as soon as it starts.
It will echo and fill the big shopping marts.
It's one of the season's most important parts.

Our feast, our feast so diverse and vast
That will sweeten the day for the entire cast.
There is plenty for all, so no one must fast.
It's for all to enjoy just like in the past.

It's Christmas, it's Christmas, the season so bright.

Embrace Your Dreams

Dreams

Nicholas, the bishop of Myra, had a very simple dream that he dared to pursue, to give the gift of giving. As a result he became St. Nicholas and much, much more. Now billions have followed and continue to follow the path of his saintly ways. He lived knowing about the unstoppable and magical power of dreams. A brief look into one small corner of his heart might read this way.

Dreams Are Magic

Dreams are magic. They make you happy.
They give you power. They give you strength.
They fill your mind and wrap your heart.
They flood your life with gifts of joy.

Add your dreams one to another.
Hear those given take them home.
Share them aloud to all those listening.
Build them strong for those who are not.

Beware the thieves who would whisk them away.
The non-believers, their numbers are great,
Fogging your path and slowing your pace.
Don't let them turn your way astray.

Nurture your dreams. Cherish their hope.
Pursue all those that lie within.
It is never too late to plant a seed.
So build your dreams. Their magic so real.

So build your dreams. They make you happy.

The First Christmas Visit

Not long ago, I received a letter. It was addressed to me but had not been mailed. I found it, or so I thought. But maybe I was supposed to find it. Maybe it was hand delivered by someone special and unique.

Let me explain.

You see, I live by myself quite far from any town or city and far off the road. It was Christmas Eve again, and I was supposed to be on my way to my parents' home to spend the holiday. That Christmas Eve, I was stuck because of a snowstorm. I had to wait till it let up so I could dig out. I went to bed early that night. I figured I would need the extra sleep to shovel mountains of snow the next day. Some Christmas Day that would make!

In the middle of my slumber, I was awakened by a noise. The wind was still blowing. Reluctantly, I got up to see what had caused the noise. Through my window, I could see snow and more snow—snow everywhere. It was falling from the sky, it covered the ground, and the wind was whipping it around in whirling clouds of white. Just then, I heard another noise coming from my roof. It sounded like several people running up there or someone dragging something across my roof—or both. It stopped suddenly, and I heard no more, but I knew I should check it out.

Once I was outside, I was quickly confused as the snow on my roof had been greatly disturbed but nothing was there. Nothing had been disturbed anywhere else. The snow in my yard still lay as Mother Nature had tossed it. The trees all around were still covered, and there were no signs of a branch coming off any of them and landing on my roof. I then laughed, thinking it was Christmas Eve and who or what would be on someone's roof except Santa Claus? Then off in the distant sky, I could see a faint red glow, as if it were coming from a small, singular light. I could also hear the jingling of bells. I stopped laughing, thinking maybe St. Nick really had been there. Nah. I went back inside and straight to bed.

In the early morning, I headed straight for the coffeemaker after waking up. With a fresh cup of coffee, I sat in front of my fireplace, preparing my mind for all the shoveling I would do that day. The rich smell of coffee was clearing my head as I thought of the past evening's events. I wondered, *Did I have a close encounter with Santa last night?* That could be a funny story to tell my family later that day. Well, it was time to get to work and dig my way out to the road.

On my way outside, I stopped and looked back at my Christmas tree. It wasn't much. It was small and lonely looking. It spent Christmas Day by itself as I was never there. That was when I noticed something under the tree: a small gift. It was tubular with wrapping and a bow. The wrapping was really quite different. It seemed made of cloth and not paper. I picked it up, confirming the wrapping was made of cloth. A Christmas winter scene adorned it. A house set in snow was decorated for Christmas. My house!

My house. How could that be? But it was.

I took my coat and boots off as I stumbled backward into my chair in front of the fireplace. Where did this gift come from? How did it get there? Who put it there? The wrapping was specially made. How was that done? It could not have been bought anywhere. It had my house stitched into the cloth. There were small beads on it, each colorful and placed to represent Christmas lights. A small name tag was attached to the gift. It was made of metal and was gold in color. Was it really gold? Someone had gone to a lot of trouble, but who and why?

Whatever was inside must be very special. The wrapping would have to come off very carefully so as to not ruin it. This was wrapping meant to be kept.

Ah, a tie string held it closed and would allow me access without ruining the cloth wrapping. It could also be retied. So I carefully, gingerly untied the string, and then I peeked inside. It looked like sheets of paper rolled in a tube. So I tilted it, allowing the papers to slide out. It was a letter of some kind. I sat there holding two letters, specially wrapped, with a golden name tag, delivered on Christmas Eve by an unknown person.

One letter was written on paper so soft yet strong that it could also be cloth. The other was on normal paper, and the sight of it was a little unnerving. I looked at this letter and read it quickly several times. I couldn't believe my eyes. This was the letter that I had written when I was very young—to Santa Claus. Not a copy. It was the original! My mind froze in time. How could this be? I had put it in a mailbox myself, expecting never to see it again, so many years ago. Yet here it was, returned to sender. That was not how it was supposed to work. After several minutes trying to gain a clear head, I read the second letter, and this led to more confusion and disbelief. It was clearly supposed to be written by Santa Claus. It had a magical script and verse. Together, they challenged my mind yet were delightful, even fun, to read.

A message from Santa Claus?

I sat there contemplating all the events. All the facts told me I had had a visit from St. Nick last night, and he had left me a gift. When you read the letters, you'll understand. My letter started, "Dear Santa," and his was entitled, "My Christmas Wish." I needed to clear my head, go outside, and get on the ugly end of my snow shovel. Besides, this would give me more time to reason this all out.

As I stepped outside onto my porch, my gaze in all directions was filled by a winter wonderland. There was deep snow everywhere. Accents of brilliant white transformed my immediate world into an artistic dream. The now-clear-blue sky allowed the sun to prism off the blankets of white snow in rainbows of color. In a glimpse, this twinkling of all the colors turned the trees of my yard into a Christmas mirage. The air was crisp and clean. I wondered, *Is this what the North Pole is like?*

I stepped off the porch, rounded the corner of my house, and was greeted by still another Christmas gift. The wind from the night before had blown the snow everywhere, but on my driveway, it had blown clear. My long day of shoveling wasn't going to happen. I chuckled and thanked the winter warlock, should he exist.

My drive that day would give some time to think about the gifts I had received and unravel who my secret Santa Claus was. After driving for maybe a half hour, I was no closer to solving my riddle. I figured I would tell my parents and siblings. After all, I figured, one of them could be behind it all. I just wanted to ignore the obvious facts that pointed straight at a visit from St. Nicholas. No way! My adult mind kept bouncing back and forth between believing in a visit from Santa and a practical joke. Which was it?

Throughout my brief Christmas holiday with my family, we talked and had fun with my experiences. My father seemed withdrawn and quiet on the matter. My siblings—all seven of them—thought I was playing a joke on them. My mother, who knew me best, believed my story and encouraged me to grasp the idea that Santa Claus had paid me a visit. If I did, then what?

They had all read the letters and suggested I had written both. As for the wrapping paper and the embroidered picture of my house on it, I was accused of making that—and the gold name tag too. They just didn't believe the story at all. Yet I was riding that fence because I was there and knew I wasn't behind any of it. By the time I left for home, I was sure none of them were either. I had figured out one thing, though. If Santa Claus wrote me a letter, it was because I wrote him and asked him to. When you read both letters, you will understand that too.

Back home again, I busied myself getting back into the routine of my life, occasionally thinking of what had happened and trying to figure out why. No one ever came forth to take credit for a practical joke, which pretty well left me with just one theory.

Dear Santa:

I know you are busy and you have lots to do, but could you give Rudolph a message for me? You see, I have listened to his song and heard his story and I know why he thinks he is a misfit.

He isn't really any different from all the rest of us. I know cause my parents told me so. You see, I am small and get picked on by bigger kids. Because of this, I used to feel really bad and thought I was a misfit. Well, I found out that a lot of kids go through times when they feel like they are misfits, and so do some adults. Rudolph is just different. That is what makes him special.

I also learned from Rudolph that my time will come. I just have to be strong. My dad says that it is when life is hard that we become stronger cause we stand up to the challenge and that is what makes us happy.

I have learned that because we are all different we are all special. My dad says that our differences makes each of us unique. Please make sure Rudolph knows this cause he is unique too. That makes him special. I like being special I hope he will too.

One more thing Santa. What do you want for Christmas?

Jimmy

My Christmas Wish

Step into Christmas. Let Suzy Snowflake touch your cheek, and let that Christmas feeling fill your heart with joy. Once a year you can forget all your troubles, even for just a while. This time of year on every street corner you can meet smile after smile, laughing all the way, bringing peace on earth. The sight of pretty paper and the sound of "Jingle Bells" lift each heart, building the twelve days of Christmas into a joyous Noel. It's the most wonderful time of the year. Oh, If every day was just like Christmas.

Looking up, my mind becomes lost in the infinite beauty of the stars and in the distance the aurora borealis. In this silent night the sound of crunching snow under each of my strides brings to mind that this is the season of joy to the world. In the lane the snow is glistening while scarlet ribbons and twinkling lights are on every Christmas tree. Santa Claus Lane brings me home to Mrs. Santa Claus and chestnuts roasting on an open fire. It's beginning to look a lot like Christmas. Let it snow! Let it snow! Let it snow! Yes, snow for Johnny.

Baby, it's cold outside. It was a night like this, in the bleak midwinter when no man but a snowman was out, that I first realized there's no place like home for the holidays, where holly leaves and Christmas trees build Christmas memories. Yes, the holy and the ivy, the little Christmas tree, the first snowfall, and toy land are a few of my favorite things. It came upon a midnight clear that it needs love to be Christmas. We need a little Christmas every year all year.

Christmas is that time of year when we celebrate our humanity and build it, contagiously. From the littlest angel to the shepherds in the field, from good Christian men to Good King Wenceslas we wish you a merry Christmas. Like Frosty the Snowman, the wonderful world of Christmas is filled with the magic of life, the greatest gift of all. The season is filled with busy sidewalks, silver bells, holly leaves, and Christmas trees, all bringing me to life. Someday at Christmas I will take a sleigh ride.

I believe the dreams of just a few have made this a special, happy holiday. From the first Noel, the celebration of just a few grew like the march of the toys, spreading good cheer and tidings of comfort and joy. Joyous voices sweet and clear joined, making spirits bright. The energy of the season will deck the halls and give me the face of jolly old Saint Nicholas. Thus I was born the way the world began. That's why people everywhere sing, "Here comes Santa Claus." Ho, ho, ho. Yes, I'll be home for Christmas. My home, your home, home for the holidays.

All I want for Christmas is for all to know that Rudolph the red-nosed reindeer pulls a sleigh because of the reality of good will. Lean your ear this way. Do you hear what I hear? Do you know what I know? I will be your Santa Claus as long as you can say, "I believe in Santa Claus."

If you welcome Christmas, the most wonderful time of the year, into your heart, then beautiful memories will be yours this Christmas, and all your Christmases will be white.

Christmas Eve is coming soon, to fill your heart with joy. Tell little Jack Frost get lost. Let there be peace on earth, and spy to see if reindeer really know how to fly. With bells on you can rejoice and be merry. All you need is a song and a Christmas tree to make this a marshmallow world. Make this a Christmas to remember and not a blue Christmas. Have a wonderful Christmastime.

While you're driving home for Christmas in a winter wonderland, you meet the nicest people every year. Do they know it's Christmas? Spread a little joy, and have a cup of cheer. Tell them of poppa Santa Claus and little Saint Nick. Sing the Christmas song for everyone to hear.

So go caroling, caroling to have yourself a merry little Christmas. When you hear the little drummer boy on a snowy Christmas night, you will know all I want for Christmas. Maybe someday you can write me and tell me a Christmas wish you have.

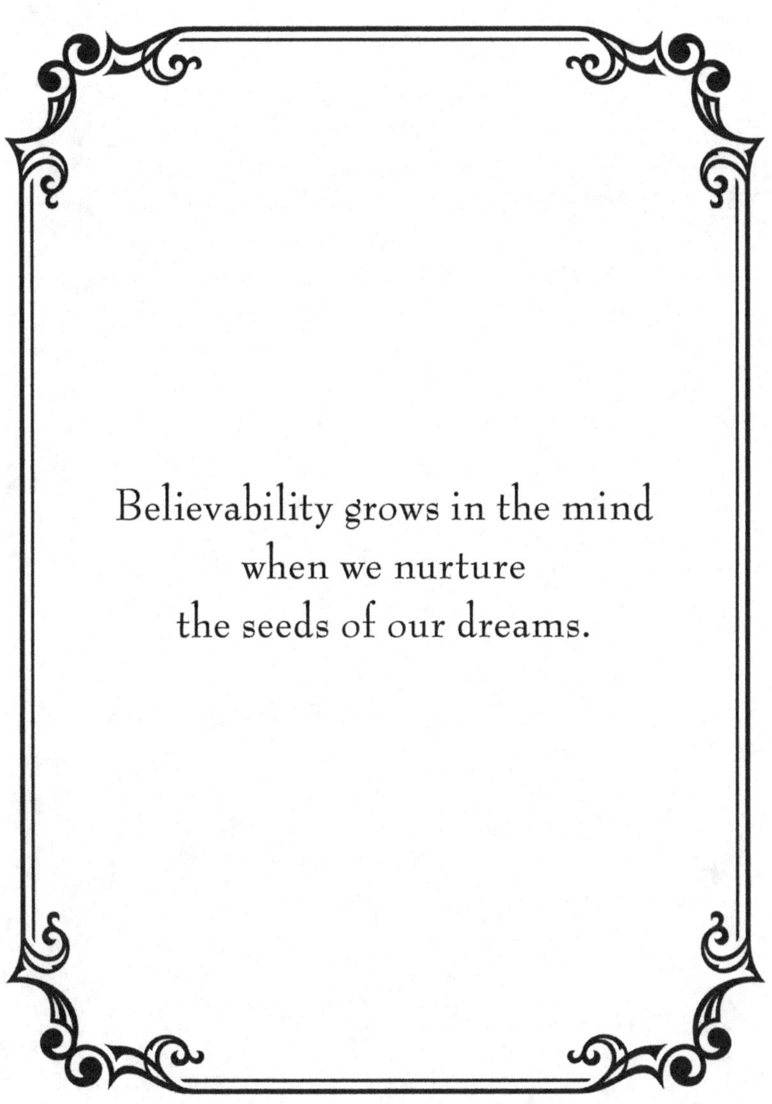

Believability grows in the mind
when we nurture
the seeds of our dreams.

The Season to Me

As the first snow falls
In many colors to white
Sidling down, in gentle flight.

My gaze grows tall,
A wondrous sight.
My world made right.

The season anon.

The winds now strong.
A storm is upon.
My calm now gone.

With blustering wind,
The drifts pile high.
I solemnly sigh.

It's winter's song.

This triggers my mind
Into glorious thought
Of what it has brought.

The Christmas rite,
The colorful lights,
The songs of delight.

A gentle smile.

We'll decorate a tree
With red, blue, and green.
It must be seen.

There will be silver and gold,
Some glass cycles too,
All shiny and new.

It waits alone.

The gifts, they will come
In pretty papers and bows.
Everything glows.

This scene to complete
For blessing the eyes
Of those little spies.

A Christmas dream.

I can picture him now,
All dressed in red,
I have heard it said.

He'll gather his team
From one to eight
Into a strong, flying gait.

On Christmas Eve,

He'll do with a smile,
With winks and nods,
The work of the gods.

The stockings he'll stuff.
The trees he'll adorn
For Christmas morn.

The chimney and flight.

That Christmas feeling,
It grows inside,
My emotions astride.

I wonder then how
To make it last.
It happens so fast.

Year after year,

I ponder the trouble,
The hustle the bustle,
My tired brain muscle.

I remember the way
Of jolly St. Nick.
I straighten up quick.

Both sides now.

He really started something
When he gave his gift,
All the world to a lift.

It will continue on
As long as we want.
Goodwill, ours to flaunt.

Christmas spirit.

I wait for this day
Year after year,
To bring good cheer.

I ponder its start
So many years ago
And where it will go.

As the wind blows
Here in the snow.

When the winds blow
Wear a hat
Under the hat
A smile!

The Second Christmas Visit

Christmas Eve had come again. I still questioned what had happen the previous year. I had spent lots of my time over the year thinking about the gift I received and the events that occurred. Here it was Christmas Eve, and for the second year in a row I had not left for my parents' house yet. This time it was not because of snow on the ground but because of the snow in my head. I had decided to stay home for that night just to see if something would happen. Then I would leave to go to my parents' house on Christmas Day.

I found it hard to go to sleep that night. Just like a little kid, I was anticipating the arrival of Santa Claus. I did not want to fall to sleep that night. If I did, I would miss his visit. I thought of sitting in my chair in front of my fireplace. Then if I fell asleep, his presence would surely wake me. Then again, I would think, I wouldn't get a good night's sleep, and that would be for nothing. Part of me was still thinking nothing was going to happen. I finally concluded I needed to quit acting like a kid and go to bed, which I did.

The next morning, I woke, rose, and headed straight for the coffeemaker. I guess that was the force of habit. I had totally forgotten why I stayed home in the first place. While waiting for the coffee, I became focused again and realized I had heard nothing the night before. I wondered if that meant no visit last night. I poured my coffee and headed to my Christmas tree. I was in no rush as I expected to see nothing there. Sauntering up to my tree and wiping my eyes, I checked under it and found nothing. I looked through the branches; nothing. I looked around the room; nothing. I finished my coffee and went outside to see if the snow on my roof had been disturbed. It was just as Mother Nature had left it.

Well, that meant my life could go back to normal. What happened last year would soon be a forgotten memory—maybe not. It was still fun to think that Santa Claus was real and that he had been to my house and wanted me to know it. Yep, at that point the whole issue was still confusing me. I needed clarity. Why me?

I dressed, packed, and started the drive to my parents' place, where they and my siblings would be waiting to hear if anything had happened between me and Santa. During the drive I realized that I would become the subject of many jokes now that nothing had happened this year. All of a sudden I wasn't looking forward to the rest of the holiday. This kinda brought whole new meaning to the song, "There is no Christmas like a home Christmas."

There I was, a Christmas traveler driving down the road, Christmas dreaming. I was thinking my only wish that year was that when I got home on Christmas Day my siblings wouldn't be waiting to heckle me. Oh well. Right about then I was thinking I'd like to hitch a ride with Santa Claus. It was Christmas. They would behave themselves, right? To break up the intensity, I started humming the song, "All I want for Christmas is my two front teeth." It gave me a small laugh.

When I arrived, everyone was quiet about the whole thing. Some of them seemed a bit tense, almost mad or upset. Something was up. Why had no one asked if anything had happened? Things were about to get worse than I thought they would. I guessed they were all waiting for me to break the ice, so I did. I explained nothing had happened. No visit. No gift. Nothing.

One of my sisters then exclaimed, "You have got to be kidding."

"Why?" I asked.

"Really!" came the reply. "I don't think this is funny anymore."

I noticed that everyone was watching and listening to us. More pointedly, all eyes were on me.

"Okay, what's going on? I don't understand. Why are you upset? What's not funny?" I asked, defending myself.

There were a few moments of quiet. My sister looked a little perplexed. I waited as she calmed down. She then asked, "I suppose you're going to tell us you had nothing to do with the gifts."

"I already told you that last year. My story stands," I calmly but assertively stated.

She drew in a breath. "Not last year's gifts—this year's gifts."

I was becoming more confused. "I also told everyone here that there were no gifts this year. Nothing happened." Her next few comments caused me to stop in disbelief.

"Not gifts to you, gifts to us--gifts to all of us. We all received gifts this year just like yours last year. We all got one of our original letters to Santa back but no other letters with them and wrapped in cloth with a picture of each of our homes on it. Just like yours. And you had nothing to do with that?"

I had to sit. I knew right then who was behind all of this. There could only be one answer. I glanced around looking for a place to sit. There was a space on the end of the sofa. I walked over to it, my head down, my mind racing. I sat down, looked up, and starting laughing. I couldn't believe the conclusion I had just drawn, but it had to be right. I suppose I was laughing in relief, yet somehow, I felt lifted.

I asked all there, looking around as I spoke, "Just how do you think I could do that? Oh, I know I stole all your letters after you mailed them and returned them decades later … for a laugh. Now that's impossible. Some of your letters were probably sent before I was born."

The room grew quiet. I could just see all their minds grappling with the facts. I asked them to check the dates on their letters. Just as I suspected, some of them were dated before I was born. Boy, there were a bunch of dim-witted looks bouncing around the room just then.

I quietly stated, "I would have to be a god to pull that off."

More silence. No one had anything to say. My emotions were busy dealing with the fact that Santa Claus had visited not once but twice. Words can't describe how great that actually felt. My sister broke the silence with an enlightened smile. "Santa Claus," was all she said. Then a few started sheepishly laughing, still not sure.

Our father walked into the room, holding a piece of paper, and asked, "How do you explain this?"

He passed the paper around the room. Each of us read it. The echoes of laughter faded completely away. The still silence was so loud it shook the room like thunder. What we had all just read, just held in our own hands, was one of our father's original letters that he had written to Santa Claus and had been returned to him like ours!

There were several minutes of silence as we all came to terms with the facts. No one dared to speak. No one knew what to say. It was proof enough, but no one was gonna believe this. Realizing that my father wrote and sent his letter decades before I was born, I broke the silence with a sarcastic quip. "Well, Dad, I had nothing to do with everybody else's letter, but I did send that one to you."

The whole room broke into laughter. It broke the tension. We were all relieved. It was the kind of shared moment and day that Christmas was all about. For a while we talked about the gifts and wondered why we had gotten them. No one could answer the nagging question—why? The funny thing was we all felt privileged for having this experience. It felt good even if we knew we couldn't tell anyone.

Later that day and out of the blue one of my brothers jokingly exclaimed, "Hey, Santa Claus, what's this all about?"

We all laughed again. We all agreed that of all the gifts we had ever gotten, these were among the best. The surprises had not come to an end yet, for later that afternoon, my mother gathered us all up and produced another gift. It was a letter she got back in the same fashion we all had but many years ago. She explained how she received her letter back even before she had started dating my father. That cinched it.

My mother got her "Dear Santa" letter returned to her about ten years after she sent it. It had no return address, just like all the rest. This all took place almost fifty years ago. She had told no one until just then. Coming forward with something like that gives you a little label. People tend to think you're a little, well, nuts.

The trip home that year was very different. I still had questions, but now I wasn't alone. By the time I arrived home, I realized I knew the "who" and the "what," but it was still hard to believe.

As for why he had come and left these gifts, well, that was gonna take some more thinking. Maybe the answer to that would come next year, or not.

The first step…

believing

Once upon a Christmas

Once upon a Christmas,
When everything was white,
I heard the sleigh bells ringing
And everything was bright.

I heard the choir singing,
Their voices sweet and clear.
I saw the children playing.
Their hearts were warm and dear.

Hats were full of magic
And Santa's reindeer too.
These images of Christmas
Help chase away the blue.

Once upon a Christmas,
When everything was new.

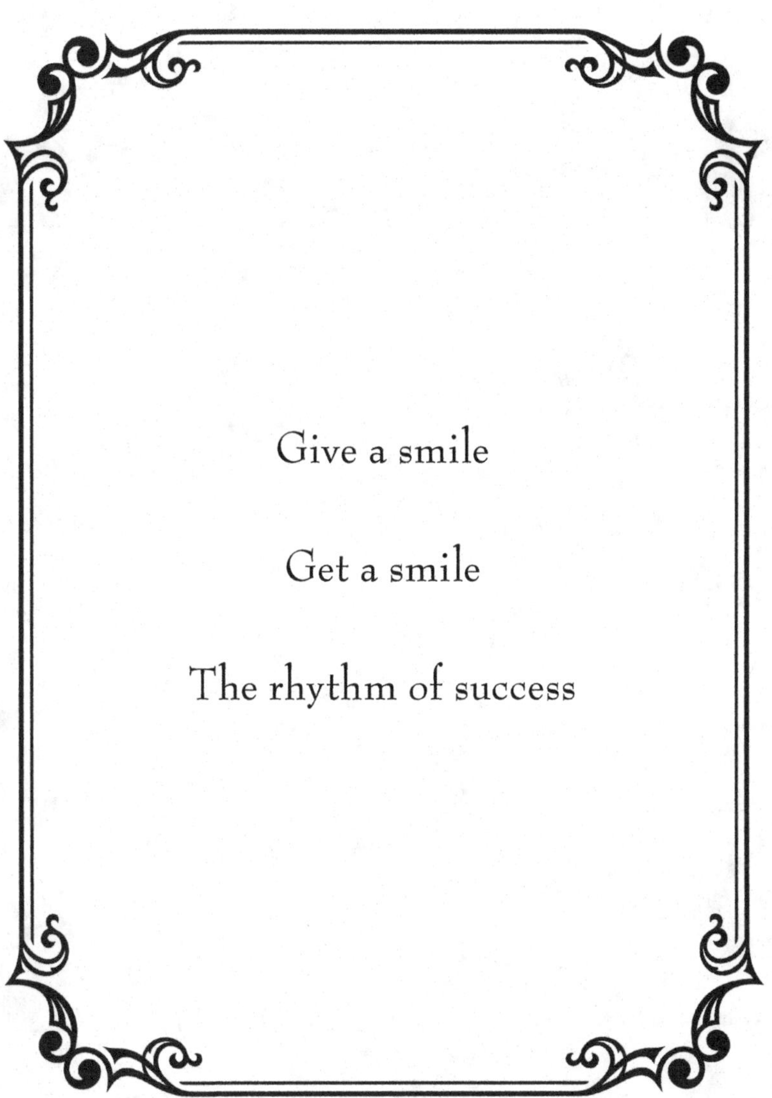

Give a smile

Get a smile

The rhythm of success

Now upon Each Christmas

Now upon each Christmas,
The memories so clear,
Knowing all the special things
That makes it all so dear.

I know about the season
And why it is so bright.
In all its special reason,
I see it black on white.

Give the gift of giving
To touch another's heart,
Then watch their passion growing.
Giving, a form of art.

Now upon each Christmas,
I send my gift to you.

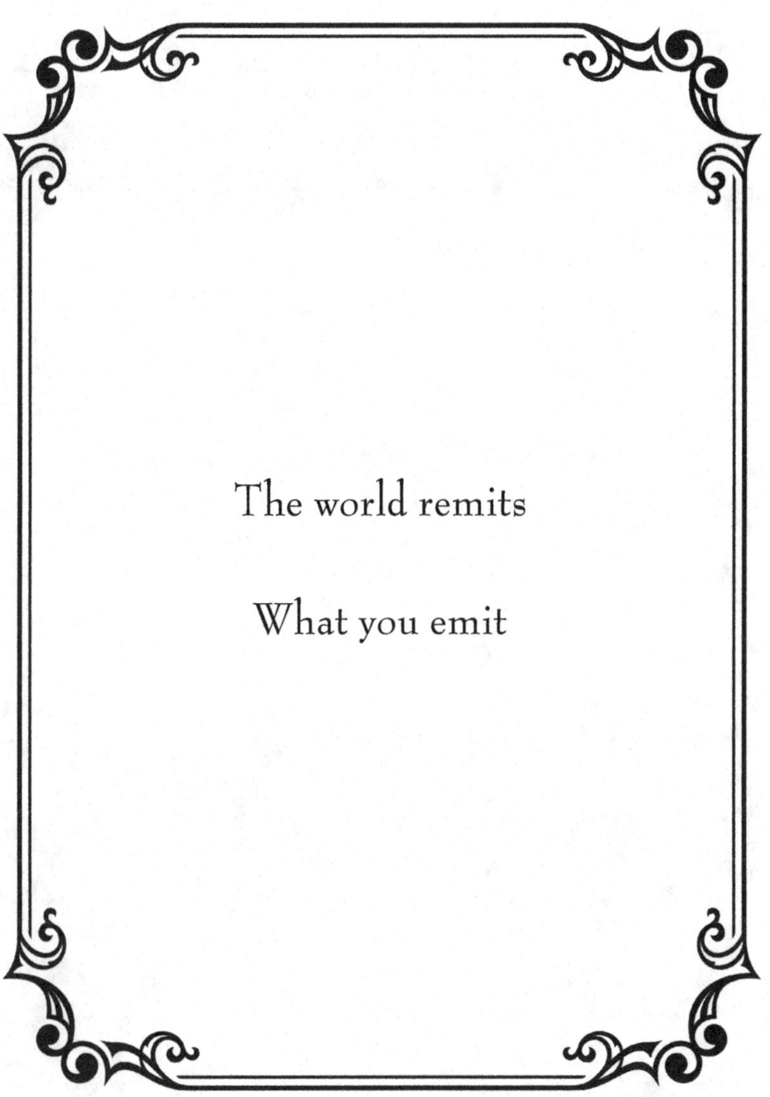

The world remits

What you emit

Now Once Each Christmas

Now once each Christmas,
I smile and celebrate,
Reflecting on my fortunes,
My day to decorate.

Now a lasting reason
To smile and celebrate,
To enjoy each holiday,
My life to decorate.

Life is but a holiday.
I search for all the white
And give the gift of giving
To make the world so bright.

Now upon each reason,
I've learned to celebrate.

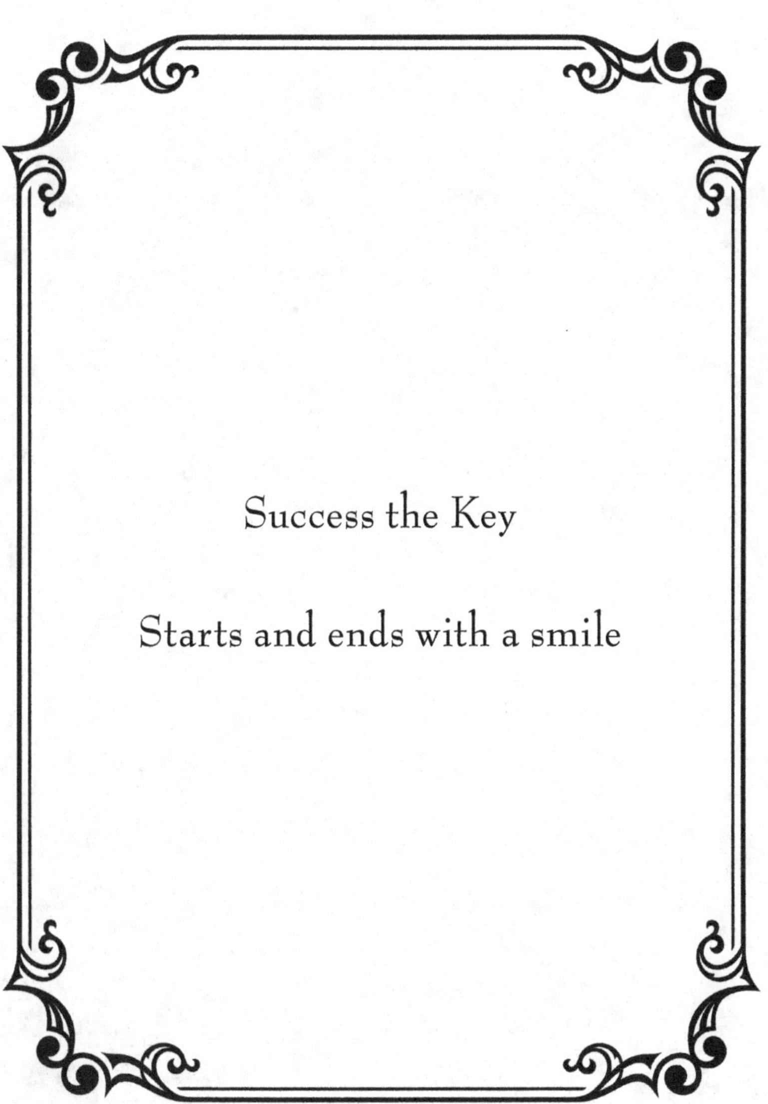

Success the Key

Starts and ends with a smile

The Journey of Nicholas

O'er the bastions of time,
To the pillars of need
In the town of Patara,
Rome's empire of greed,
Came an island of hope
For Nicholas to lead.

From the eye of his heart
And the want of his love,
He gave of his gold
And opened his glove
To those in great need
As though from above.

He journeyed to Myra,
Made bishop by name,
Where he gave of himself
To those of no blame.
For his endless bounty
Came saintly acclaim.

From bishop to saint,
A step of change.
St. Nicholas abounds,
A person of range,
His journey to take,
The way to arrange.

He traveled far north,
New friends to greet,
Their enchanting gifts
A magical treat.
Side by side,
They all took a seat.

Working their craft,
The miracle of giving.
Just once in twelve
On an eve for living,
He tends to the list
Of those most giving.

In a sleigh of bright red,
He takes to the sky,

His sack full of toys
So wee hearts will fly.
On his reindeer of eight
He must surely rely.

Dare To Do

The Songs of Christmas

(Music of the Heart)

Sing the songs of Christmas.
Sing them all year long.
They lend us much learning.
In your heart grow strong.
Fill your lifelong yearnings
And feel the good in all.
Let the music echo o'er the year a call.

Reflect and keep.
Worship deep.
All the days you are,
Through Father's Day and Mother's Day
To birthdays and more,
Hear the songs of Christmas.
Ply their special greetings
So e'er your heart be warm.

The universal language,
The music of the heart.

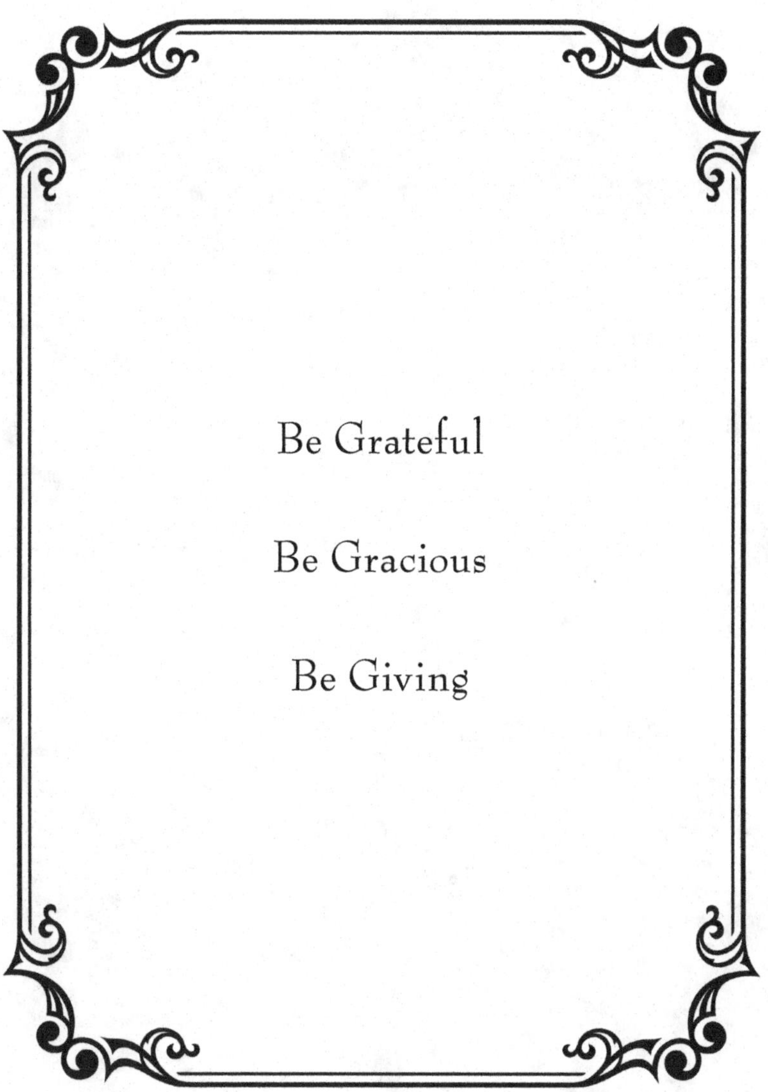

Be Grateful

Be Gracious

Be Giving

The Third Christmas Visit

Christmas was just around the corner, and as you might think, I had spent much more time that year thinking of the gifts and Christmas. I was in contact with my family much more that year. We all agreed that Christmas, especially the last two, had brought us all closer to one another—just like it was supposed to do. I often thought of my mother, who kept her secret for almost fifty years. How did she do that? I didn't last one day before I told my family. Maybe it all leads to me and the fact that I would tell people. I am a writer. That's what I do. Interesting. I had been writing lots that past year about Christmas.

That Christmas I was wondering if anything was going to happen at all. After all, each one of us had gotten a letter back, just like my mother, and she never got anything ever again. But then why would Santa do that? It just didn't make any sense. I guessed we were all going to have to wait to see what happened. That Christmas Eve I sat at home writing about Christmas, something I had never done before on Christmas Eve. When I tired, I put the poem I was writing on my desk with a bunch of other things I had written and went off to bed.

The next morning I woke to find the strangest thing. Neatly placed under my Christmas tree were some of my written works and some new stuff, which I assumed were written by Kris Kringle. Mine had been removed from my desk and placed there by someone other than me. That had to have been done by just one person, or should I say saint. I paused and looked at them, wondering if they had been placed in any special pattern. Each story or poem laid face up and separated from the next with a blank piece of paper. That told me that there was some significance to the way they were laid out or that I was to pause first and then pick them up. I got out my camera and took a picture of exactly how they laid. I later realized I was to fill the blank pieces of paper by writing myself.

As I looked at the first paper, something I wrote, it was still a work in progress. I had not even given it a title yet. It was not a typical goodwill Christmas message. I read it even though I had written it.

A pessimist is someone who looks at the negative in something then decides to do nothing, as it is hopeless in his or her mind.
An optimist is someone who looks at the positive in something then decides to act, not fearing mistakes or failure knowing they are the stepping stones of success.
A realist is someone who looks at something then decides to be an optimist or a pessimist.
The trick is not to hide behind being a realist, thus becoming a pessimist.
Realize your limits but search to stretch them.

I had been contemplating, the day I wrote it, about positive thinkers and negative thinkers. I was surrounded by both and wondered about the few who called themselves realists. I watched them over the years. I noticed that most of the realists made a list of the pros and the cons in every situation, and no matter how much the pros outweighed the cons, their decisions were made in favor of the cons. That really made them pessimists. However, there were a few who found the positive almost always and then moved ahead, using it as their guide or solace. In order to succeed in life, I needed to be more of an optimist. I knew I had my share of bad luck and had made some dandy mistakes. But I also realized everyone else has bad luck and made mistakes too. In order for me to move on, no matter how difficult things became, I could only be happy if I looked for the brighter side in everything.

When my wife was taken from us unexpectedly, I realized that she would not want me to go through the rest of my life unhappy. The first positive thing I started to focus on was that she would want me to be happy and remember the good times we had. I owed it to her and to me to look for the brighter side of what had happened, so I did. So Father Christmas was telling me to be positive—about what?

The next thing I read was a very short poem I wrote:

The road is long,
The hill steep.
Inhale deep,
Then move along.

My mother had another way of putting that. She used to say, "When the going gets tough, the tough get going."

Boy, I had really gotten the feeling that I was about to be asked to something very difficult.

The third item I read was not written by me but left and written by Poppa Santa Claus:

You have been asked
To do a task.
You see it hard.
You know not why.
You know not how.
Take a deep breath.
Do what you love.
Do.
Do what you do best.
Do.

That was pretty straightforward to me. Poppa Santa Claus wanted me to write about Christmas and him, but why me?

Many nights after that I sat in my chair in front the fireplace writing about Christmas and what it meant.

I would also wonder, why me? I reasoned that many people before me had written and sang about Christmas, and some of them may have been asked to just like me. It would be a clever way for Santa to get his message out. Think about it. All those songs, movies, television specials, poems, and books were written by people who could have been directly inspired by jolly old St. Nicholas. Then I stopped to realize he was definitely influencing them indirectly.

I believe that Santa Claus is the physical manifestation of the spirit of Christmas. The spirit of Christmas is huge; it touches and has touched billions of people. All those people who have written, sang, danced, or even dreamt about Christmas have done so and will continue to do so because that spirit has touched them inside. It is their inspiration. It is contagious.

So Saint Nicholas was asking me to join the ranks of many by writing about Christmas and him. The hard part would be telling about the letters and how they came. Some people would laugh.

Then I realized, just as he had written, that it would be easy if I just wrote it in a book. So I did. Looking back, I was unknowingly doing that before his first visit. I wonder if he knew that too.

For the third year in a row on Christmas Day, I got into my car and drove to my parents' home to celebrate the holiday with my family. I felt sorry for those around the world who were not able to spend the holiday with their family and friends. I wondered what my reception would be like when I got there and if anybody got a gift that year other than me. Christmas carols played on the radio all the way there. They had an even greater meaning to me now and would for the rest of my life.

Arriving at my parents', I found that I was the only one who received anything that year. Through the course of that holiday, we discussed the gifts of all three years and what they meant. My mother pointed out that we were all given the gifts because that is what we all had done all our lives. Each one of us gave to our families, our friends, our work, and our communities. She believed and had taught us that you got the best that life had to offer by giving to others and that if you gave to others, you would receive life's special gifts. She surmised that our gifts from Saint Nicholas were just such gifts, but it was my turn to give again by writing.

My drive home became a good example of that. As I was driving home, I came upon an older couple who got their car stuck in the snow. They were too old to get out and shovel or to walk anywhere on a cold night like that. They were stuck and in a bad way. I stopped and started to dig them out. As we were struggling to get them out, the odd car went by, but no one stopped to help. I felt sad for those who didn't stop. They were missing out on life's best because obviously there were not giving. After almost a half hour of digging and pushing, the old couple were free and on their way. I felt pretty good for them and proud of my efforts. I finished my drive home quite happily, thinking how good it felt to give.

A few days later, a very large gift basket came to my door. It was full of snacks and treats. It was addressed to me but signed by no one. There was a note attached that read, "We are home safe and sound. We will always remember the stranger who helped us one snowy winter night."

All this comes easy to the family of Kringle.

Kringles Are

When you place upon a tree
A star to shine, all will see.
It shimmers there because of thee,
A gift from you on bended knee.

You've put it there for hearts to glow.
This is so your mind will know.
Your heart is in a warming flow
And for gifts a place below.

Like a Kringle.

You do for them who need of you.
Upon your face a smile, tis true.
Because their lives are made anew,
When you give to them to woo.

You always share all your joy.
To touch a soul is your ploy.
With all your heart you employ,

To give a child a shining toy.

Like a Kringle.

Just like Santa's little elves,
Who place the gifts upon his shelves.
They give so much of themselves,
So our souls into Christmas delve.

They who help the Christmas Kris
Do with him all of this.
They join him in his annual bliss
To give a day a Christmas kiss.

Like a Kringle.

If you find you do all this,
Welcome to the family of Kringle.

Why

Over the years, I have thought about these letters and events and how initially I struggled to buy into the idea that Santa Claus really existed and how fast that had changed. A curious thing—even before I got my first gift of letters, I had occasionally taken out my pad and written about Christmas, some of which you have already read. They represent the thoughts etched in the minds of some of our world. I write because I feel compelled to do so as St. Nicholas asked me to. I think even greater than that is my desire to give something to this world that would help it … my desire to give. Maybe my dream will grow too. After all, my dream is nothing more than an extension of his and many others. I wonder, does St. Nicholas know all this and that is why he chose me?

These letters lead me to ask one question, assuming they have been given to me from Father Christmas. Why did he take so long to answer mine? I realized that he has been around for a long time and as such he would have great wisdom. With that wisdom, he realized timing is everything. In order for me to get his message out as he asked, I would need the means and the ability to do so. I have acquired both; after all, you are reading his message now.

Father Christmas has a twinkle in his eye,
Something to him over many years.
His gaze is deep and his smile profound,
His tacit voice for all our ears.

He can speak in rhyme
And right across time.
His message so deep.
It is ours to keep.

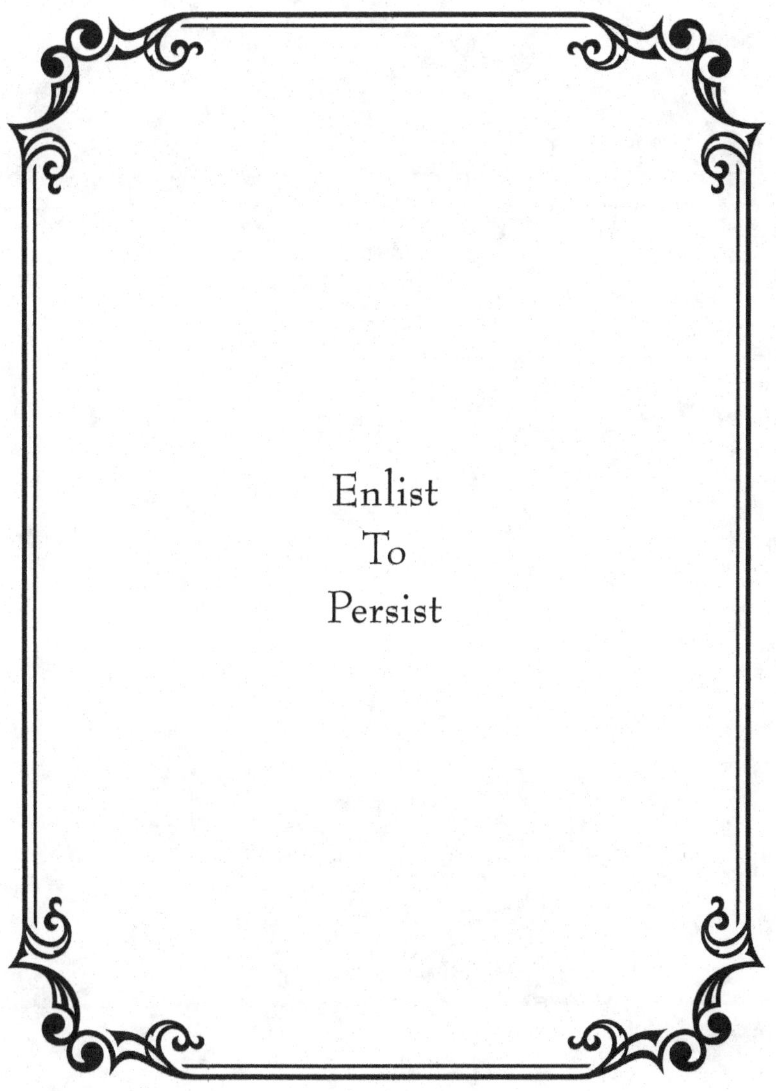

Enlist
To
Persist

Poppa Santa Claus

Poppa Santa Claus is a stoutly figure.
He lays his finger aside his nose.
He winks and nods in a smiling pose,
Then up the chimney he goes.

Upon each year, he is eager with task,
Delivering gifts, how long will this last?
All through the night, just like in the past,
His job so great and really quite vast.

His turn in this role a valiant cause.
Renowned is his way and saintly name.
He bears with honor his lineage of fame.
He reads each list, to him not a game.

He learned his trade, his place in time,
The gathering of gifts to load his sleigh,
To stop at each house those on his way,
To make it all pass in fun and play.

He ponders his family tree.
Its roots are long so all can see.
He'll pause one day on just one knee
And give his guidance to little Saint Nick.

Poppa Santa Claus is a fatherly figure.

Christmas Is?

Over the years, I have realized that Christmas is not just a holiday for children or for just the child in all of us. It can mean many things if you let it. This too I learned by observing those around me and those I have met throughout my life. Christmas means so many different things to so many different people. It is not just a day to some, nor is it a just a season. There are the lucky ones who take the true meaning of Christmas and have made it a part of their everyday life.

Within the pages of this book, the foundation for that type of life has been laid out as I have observed it from the lucky ones. When you have read it once, take some time to read it again. You may learn even more and enjoy it even more each time you read it. I wrote it, but I still read it quite often because like beauty, you see it as you are and not how it is. Beauty is in the eye of the beholder. Therefore, as your wisdom grows throughout your life, what you draw from this book will grow too. One will feed the other.

I have been very fortunate in my life to have met many people who understand and live their lives through the gift of giving. Many did not learn it just from their experiences with Christmas. They do, however, understand how that is not just what Christmas is truly all about but rather that is what life is all about. It doesn't matter where they live, the color of their skin, or how rich they are they live that code and are truly happy because they make those around them happy.

These lucky souls are like seeds of grass; where there is one there are many. As they go through life planting the seeds of this knowledge, they are joined by others who already new the secret of Christmas or have learned it from them. I have met many such seeds. I heard long ago that a person can be a "good seed." Now I know what that really means.

To become such a seed is really quite simple. Figuratively speaking, all you have to do is to do what I did—join the family of Kringle.

Read Anew

Read Anon

The Secret Of Christmas

Let me tell you a secret I know—a secret passed on over hundreds of years. Whether it is fact or fiction is not important, but what is important is that the fiction became fact.

How I learned the secret is hard to believe, but that's not important. The message of the secret is. I do know that it has been entrusted to many over the years. Who the others are I do not know. I suspect many. I just know it came to me a little at a time, and now it is time for me to pass it on.

You see at first and for a while I started having dreams and ideas that were random and seemed not linked in any way. Then over the years, the dreams became bigger and started to repeat themselves. Then I started to form ideas. The ideas were about the dreams, and they started to make sense of the dreams. But why over years? I do not know. Maybe that's the way it is for everybody who learns the secret.

The first dreams were just of the desire to give to others. I know that's not unusual. Lots of people do that. Looking back, though, that was my first clue to knowing that I was not the first person to learn the secret. Then I learned that there is a master at the art of giving, and he has been doing it for hundreds of years. He has a system, a procedure, and lots of help. Some of those who choose to help him may not even realize they are. They just want to give and watch others receive. That could be catching and get to be very big. It did.

Oh, so you have had the same dreams and ideas I've had. You are learning the secret the same way I did. Now you know the first part of the secret—the desire to give. Yep, it's common knowledge yet often forgot and misunderstood. That is the start of the fiction becoming fact.

Now you ask, "Who is this master, and how did he get started?" Well, his name is Nicholas, the bishop of Myra, and he started the same way you and I did. He had a dream and then some ideas. Then he decided to make his dream of giving to others a reality. Now who said dreams don't come true? In this case, it is a historic fact.

Nicholas soon learned that he couldn't give to all those he wanted to without help, if his dream was that of a saint. He just needed a little help, and that is exactly what he got at first—lots of little helpers. It was a family, you might say. His helpers were just like him. They liked to give too, but they had something else to offer. They were craftsmen who made things, small things like jewelry, little knickknacks, and toys.

As the years went by, their little enterprise grew, and soon it was so big they couldn't keep up, so they decided they were only going to give the gifts once a year. Well, they had to make lots of changes to meet the growing needs.

The thing is that no normal person could do all this and neither could Nicholas, even though all his efforts were saintly. The thing about saintly deeds is they have power. They start out with just the power of love. The more that power is used, the bigger it gets, and the stronger it gets. The stronger it gets, the more you know it is real. If a person does enough saintly deeds, he or she can become a saint.

Our world was created this very way. Our greatest minds tell us our world began when the power of energy created the first solid piece of our world. This small beginning created everything we know--enough of the science lesson. In years to come, you will learn this, if you don't already know it. The point is Nicholas became Saint Nicholas the same way the world began. The power and energy of his love of giving grew and grew until Nicholas the bishop of Myra became Saint Nicholas. That is the second way fiction became fact.

But for now, more about the power of Saint Nicholas or some say his magic. There is a belief that if you put enough dreamers in the same room, they will make their dreams come true—fiction becoming fact. The power of their dreams can grow and grow so that it has a magical power all its own, as Nicholas became Saint Nicholas. Saint Nicholas became many things to many people and took on many faces. He is known by many names: Father Christmas, Sinterklaas, Christkind, Kris Kringle, and Santa Claus, to name a few.

With all this power that we call magic given to him, Santa Claus does unbelievable things, like make reindeer fly.

You laugh. Let me guess—you have never seen one fly, and you don't know anybody who has. Therefore, according to you, reindeer can't fly and there is no such thing as Santa Claus, yet millions do believe. There are more believers than nonbelievers. That's why the Christmas season gets bigger and bigger every year.

Maybe you should think about it this way. You can't feel love, nor can you see it, if you don't believe in it. Yet almost all of us believe in love and its magic. Those who believe in love can feel it and see its results without ever seeing love itself. It is sad that some people don't believe in love, yet all of us have experienced it whether we know it or not. Some people know about love but not Santa Claus. Santa Claus is love—the manifestation of one form of love. Does he have a physical body like us? That would make him human, and we already know he is a saint.

I find it incredible that we all believe in all manner of things that we cannot see, but some don't believe in Santa Claus because they haven't seen him. Further, they laugh at and scoff at people who do believe in him. How about the South Pole? Do you believe it exists? Then why not the North Pole—Santa's North Pole? I'll bet you that you will never see either, but you don't believe in just the latter. Can you see the electricity that flows through the wires in the walls of your home? Funny thing, you can feel electricity. Well, you can feel Santa too. How about light? It's the very thing that allows us to see, yet we can't see it but we believe in it.

There all kinds of things that we cannot see but we believe are real. We believe in them, but some don't believe in Santa Claus because they have never seen him. Yet every year billions see the results and feel the results of him and his elves. For those who believe, the seeing is in the believing.

But more about Santa's helpers, his elves. They soon needed helpers too. These helpers bring Christmas joy to those around them every year but never think of themselves as Santa's helpers. Every year they pick up the torch and make sure those they love experience the wonders of getting a gift while they take great joy in the giving. Now does that sound like anyone you know? Maybe that is Santa Claus guiding you to give. You may have just experienced fiction becoming fact. I hope that felt good. This is the third example of the fiction becoming fact.

Let's get back to those reindeer and oh yes, the sleigh they pull. We should probably also talk about the chimney thing too. I constantly hear reindeer can't fly. "They don't have wings." Of course they don't have wings. Then they would be birds. Lots of things fly that don't have wings, like baseballs, rockets, sound, and even ideas. Have you ever heard the phrase, "The idea just flew around the room"? Well, lots of people have seen that happen, and the rest of us just believe it happens. So don't let someone tell you reindeer can't fly just because they have never seen them or because they don't have wings.

Santa has a sleigh. Of course he does. Let's just look at the facts. Santa has been doing his Christmas Eve deliveries for hundreds of years. He lived then and still does live at the North Pole. Now with all that snow and ice, what better way to get around with a big red sack full of goodies than in a sleigh? Of course he would have to use reindeer to pull his sleigh; he couldn't use camels at the North Pole. Can they fly? Don't forget the powers of saints.

One of the biggest questions about Santa Claus is how does a big jolly man go down chimneys? The answer to that is easy. A man can't go up and down chimneys, but Santa is a saint with saintly powers, remember! This is the fourth part of the fiction becoming fact.

Here is the fifth and last part of how fiction has become fact. Santa exists today and will forever as long as people believe in him. Millions of people all around the world love and believe in Santa Claus by any of his names. It is our love and our need of him and what he does that brings him to life. It is all that power, that energy that comes together, and that makes something out of nothing. Something like the way the world began. Ask your science teacher about that.

In five short steps, you have learned the five ways in which fiction became fact. They are the five secrets of Christmas. They are precious like gold. They work together and go on in unending circles like five golden rings. That's why at Christmastime the people of Christmas sing of "five golden rings." Now you know why, and if you listen each year, at Christmas you will hear voices singing, "five golden rings."

There are two things about the "the secret of Christmas." The first is that Christmas has many secrets. The second and most wondrous secret of Christmas is understanding the power of our belief in Christmas! It is the energy that has made it all real.

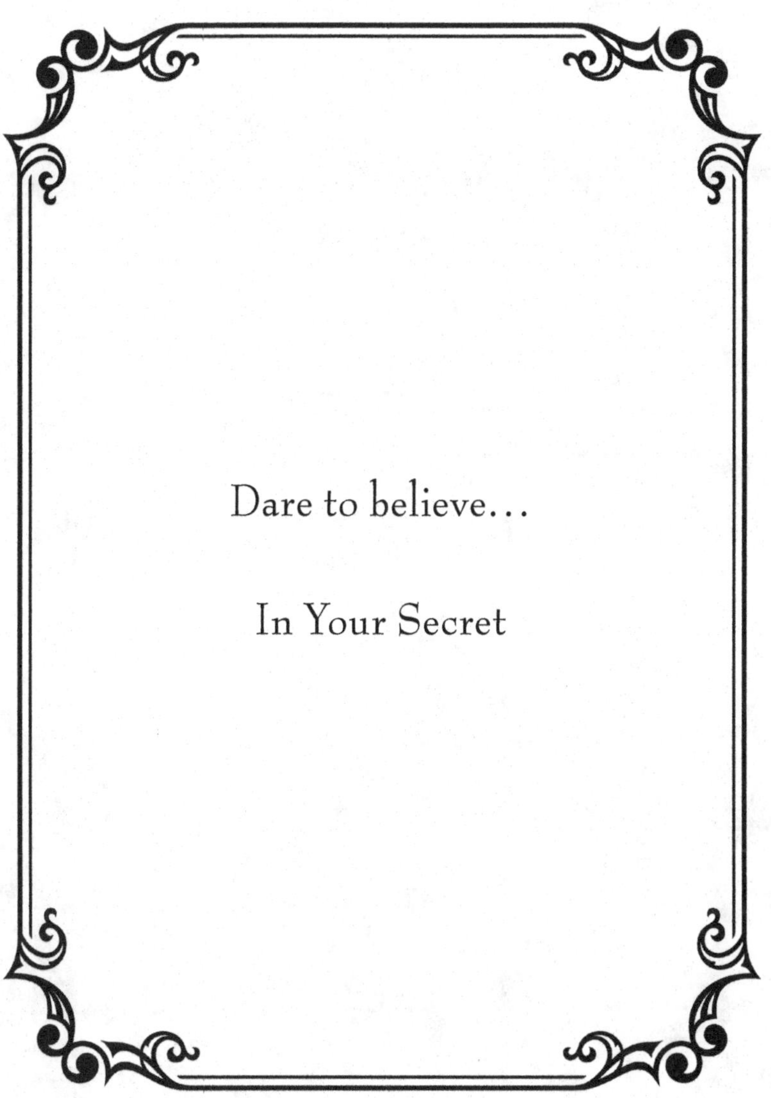
Dare to believe…
In Your Secret

Appreciate

Christmas is a season,
Just one of many.
Christmas is a reason,
Just one of many,
To reach a deep and inner peace.

Friends are so pleasin',
No matter how many.
Family are a reason,
No matter how many,
To greet each heart with a smile.

Listen for the bells.
Their tones are many.
Their joy it wells
In tones of many,
To ring the sound of joyous mirth.

Hear the Christmas story.
Make it one of many.
Celebrate in glory

In days of many,
To lift each day in chimes of cheer.

Christmas is the reason
To celebrate,
The many seasons
To celebrate,
Each and every day
To appreciate.

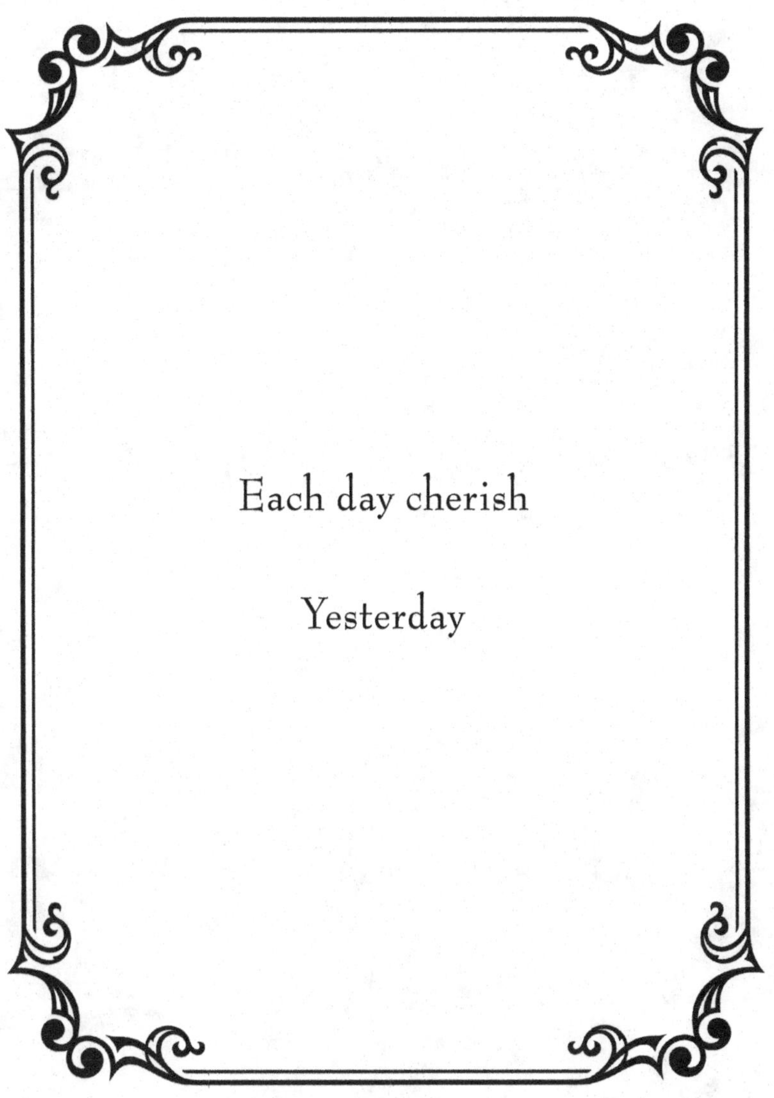

Each day cherish

Yesterday

Snows of the Sun

The snowflakes of life will fall against your door.
Some will pile high across your path.
Some will come softly falling gently at your feet.
Others will drift deeply challenging your will.
No matter who you are, the snows will come.
Old Man Winter touches everyone.

It is part of life.

The warm winter sun will shine on you.
It can peek through clouds and warm your day.
It can shine long and strong, reaching deep inside.
On sunny days, our life is good, our path at ease.
No matter who you are, the sun will come.
Fun in the sun touches everyone.

It is part of life.

Look for the sun reach for its rays.
They come in many shapes to ease your way.
To end your sadness, search for a smile.
Even a small one can turn your day.
No matter how hard, search for the sun.

It is the only way it touches everyone.

It is part of life.

The snows of life have many sides.
You cannot choose when they will come.
You can only choose to see their beauty.
Make each storm a chance for a smile.
No matter the weather, laugh just for fun.
Weather the weather, it touches everyone.

It is the cycle of life … snow into sun.

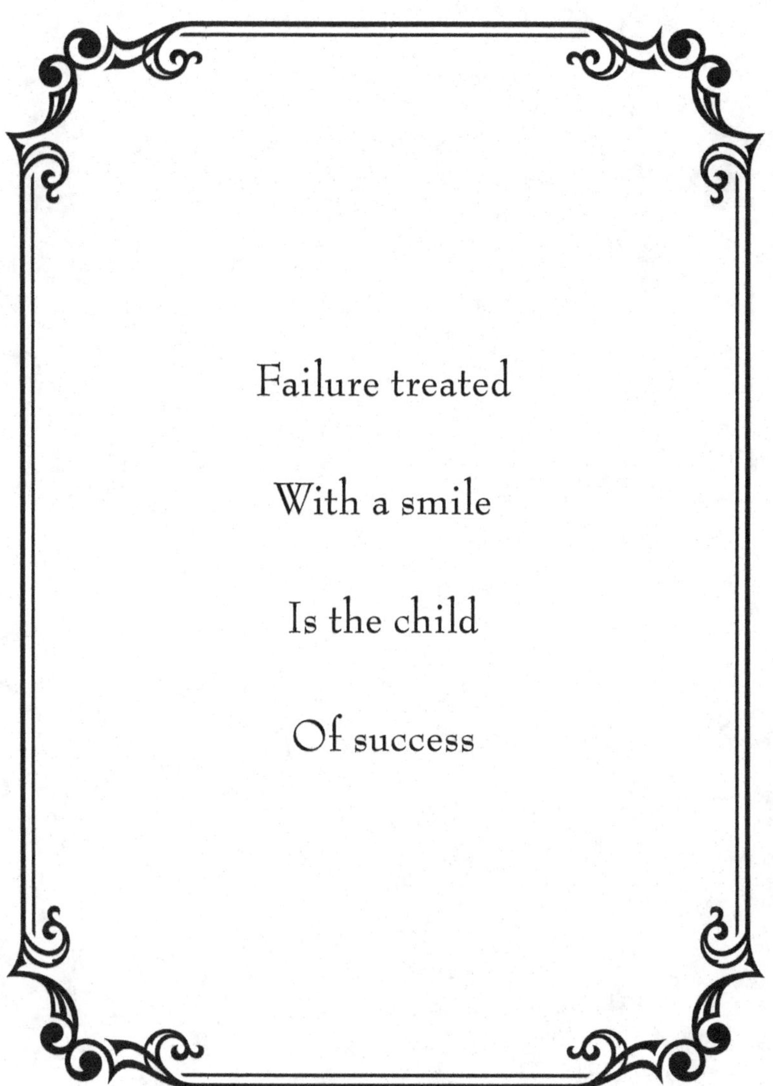

Failure treated

With a smile

Is the child

Of success

Appreciate Snows of the Sun

Christmas is a season,
Just one of many.
Christmas is a reason,
Just one of many,
To reach a deep and inner peace.

The snowflakes of life will fall against your door.
Some will pile high across your path.
Some will come softly, falling gently at your feet.
Others will drift deeply, challenging your will.
No matter who you are, the snows will come.
Old Man Winter touches everyone.

It is part of life.

Friends are so pleasin',
No matter how many.
Family are a reason,
No matter how many,
To greet each heart with a smile.

The warm winter sun will shine on you.
It can peek through clouds and warm your day.
It can shine long and strong, reaching deep inside.
On sunny days, our life is good, our path at ease.
No matter who you are, the sun will come.
Fun in the sun touches everyone.

It is part of life.

Listen for the bells.
Their tones are many.
Their joy it wells,
In tones so many,
To ring the sound of joyous mirth.

Look for the sun reach for its rays.
They come in many shapes to ease your way,
To end your sadness search for a smile.
Even a small one can turn your day.
No matter how hard, search for the sun.
It is the only way it touches everyone.

It is part of life.

Hear the Christmas story.
Make it one of many.
Celebrate in glory,
In days of many,
To lift each day in chimes of cheer.

The snows of life have many sides.
You cannot choose when they will come.
You can only choose to look to their beauty.
So make each storm a chance for a smile.

No matter the weather, laugh just for fun.
Weather the weather, it touches everyone.

It is the cycle of life ... snow into sun.

Christmas is a reason
To celebrate.
The many seasons
To celebrate.
Each and every day
To appreciate.

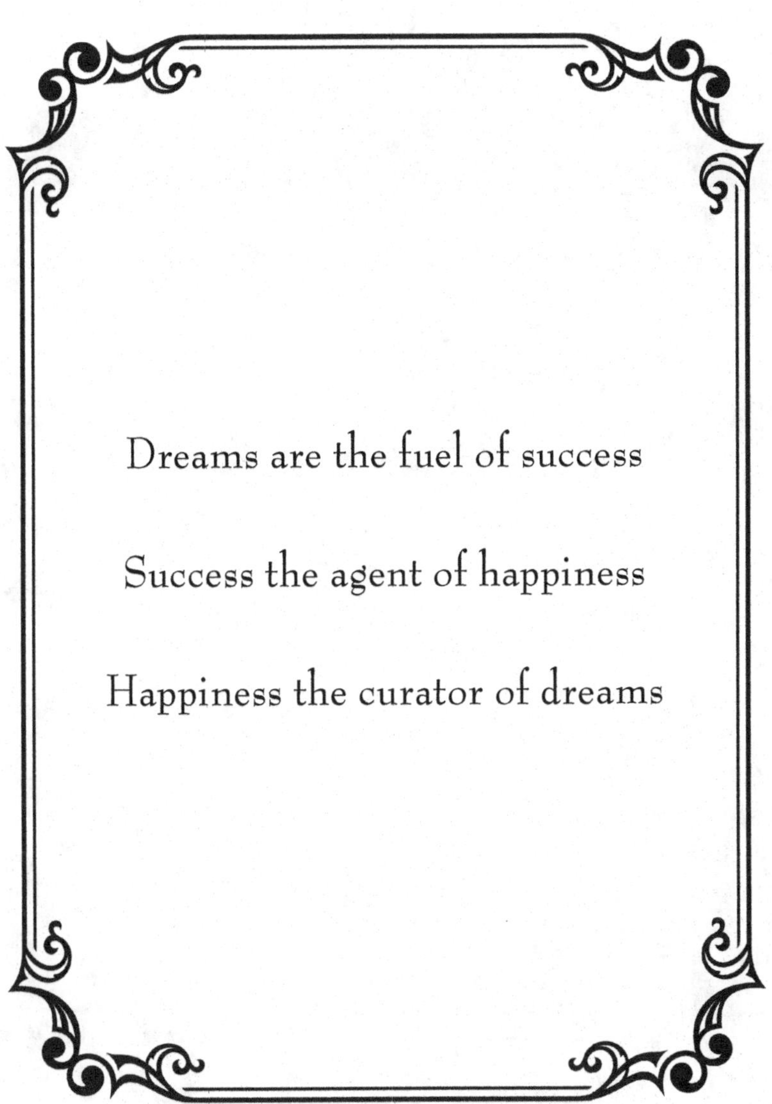

Dreams are the fuel of success

Success the agent of happiness

Happiness the curator of dreams

Giving

You must give your glass water before you can drink from it.

Giving has blessed our world.
It makes us happy.
Giving will soothe our world.
Giving will nurse our world.
It is all …
Giving has built our world.

The one thing we all have—to give.

Author Biography

Over many decades James Marion King has observed, learned and used tools of success that he has learned from many successful people. He has failed his way to success many times using these tools. He has taught hundreds and now passes on some of that knowledge to you.

Printed in the United States
By Bookmasters